AF538259

ASPATORE
C-Level Business Intelligence™

ASPATORE
C-Level Business Intelligence™

Praise for Books, Briefs, Journals & Guides:

"What C-Level executives read to keep their edge and make pivotal business decisions. Timeless classics for indispensable knowledge." - Richard Costello, Manager-Corporate Marketing Communication, General Electric (NYSE: GE)

"True insight from the doers in the industry, as opposed to the critics on the sideline." - Steve Hanson, CEO, On Semiconductor (NASDAQ: ONNN)

"Unlike any other business books, Inside the Minds captures the essence, the deep-down thinking processes, of people who make things happen." - Martin Cooper, CEO, Arraycomm

"The only useful way to get so many good minds speaking on a complex topic." - Scott Bradner, Senior Technical Consultant, Harvard University

"What the bigwigs read." - Paul Simons, CEO, Ogilvy & Mather UK

"Easy, insightful reading that can't be found anywhere else." - Domenick Esposito, Vice Chairman, BDO Seidman

"A rare peek behind the curtains and into the minds of the industry's best." - Brandon Baum, Partner, Cooley Godward

"Intensely personal, practical advice from seasoned dealmakers." - Mary Ann Jorgenson, Coordinator of Business Practice Area, Squire, Sanders & Dempsey

"Become an expert yourself by learning from experts." Jennifer Openshaw, Founder, Women's Financial Network, Inc.

"An informative insider's perspective." - Gary Klotz, Labor & Employment Law Practice Group Manager, Butzel Long

"A quick and comprehensive view of the key challenges and outlook....by the some of the best in the business." - Satish Gupta, CEO, Cradle Technologies

"Real advice from real experts that improves your game immediately." - Dan Woods, CTO, Capital Thinking

"Get real cutting edge industry insight from executives who are on the front lines." - Bob Gemmell, CEO, Digital Wireless

"An unprecedented collection of best practices and insight..." - Mike Toma, CTO, eLabor

"A snapshot of everything you need to know about the industry/profession." - Jack Guedj, President, Tvia

"Must have information for business executives." - Alex Wilmerding, Principal, Boston Capital Ventures

"An important read for those who want to gain insight....lifetimes of knowledge and understanding..." - Anthony Russo, Ph.D., CEO, Noonan Russo Communications

"A tremendous treasure trove of knowledge...perfect for the novice or the seasoned veteran."- Thomas L. Amberg, CEO, Cushman Amberg Communications

"A snapshot of everything you need..." - Charles Koob, Co-Head of Litigation Department, Simpson Thacher & Bartlett

"A wealth of real world experience from the acknowledged industry leaders you can use in your own business." - Doug Cavit, CTO, McAfee.com

"Great practical advice and thoughtful insights." - Mark Gruhin, Partner, Schmeltzer, Aptaker & Shepard, P.C.

INSIDE THE MINDS

Empowering Professionals of All Levels With C-Level Business Intelligence

www.InsideTheMinds.com

The critically acclaimed *Inside the Minds* series provides readers of all levels with proven business intelligence from C-Level executives (CEO, CFO, CTO, CMO, Partner) from the world's most respected companies. Each chapter is comparable to a white paper or essay and is a future-oriented look at where an industry/profession/topic is heading and the most important issues for future success. Each author has been carefully chosen through an exhaustive selection process by the *Inside the Minds* editorial board to write a chapter for this book. *Inside the Minds* was conceived in order to give readers actual insights into the leading minds of business executives worldwide. Because so few books or other publications are actually written by executives in industry, *Inside the Minds* presents an unprecedented look at various industries and professions never before available. The *Inside the Minds* series is revolutionizing the business book market by To nominate yourself, another individual, or a group of executives for an upcoming Inside the Minds book, or to suggest a specific topic for an Inside the Minds book, please email jason@aspatore.com.

For information on bulk orders, sponsorship opportunities or any other questions, please email store@aspatore.com.

For information on licensing the content in this book, or any content published by Aspatore, please email jennifer@aspatore.com.

To nominate yourself, another individual, or a group of executives for an upcoming Inside the Minds book, or to suggest a specific topic for an Inside the Minds book, please email jason@aspatore.com.

www.Aspatore.com

Aspatore publishes only the biggest names in the business world, including C-Level leaders (CEO, CTO, CFO, COO, CMO, Partner) from over half the world's 500 largest companies and other leading executives. By focusing on publishing only C-Level executives, Aspatore provides professionals of all levels with proven business intelligence from industry insiders, rather than relying on the knowledge of unknown authors and analysts. Aspatore publishes a highly innovative line of business intelligence publications including Inside the Minds, Bigwig Briefs, ExecRecs, Business Travel Bible (BTB), Brainstormers, IdeaJournal, CareerJournal and Aspatore Business Reviews, in addition to other best selling business books, journals and briefs. Aspatore focuses on publishing traditional print books with individuals, while our portfolio companies, Corporate Publishing Group (B2B agent & publisher) and ExecEnablers (business intelligence stores) focus on developing areas within the business and book publishing worlds. Aspatore is committed to providing our readers, authors, bookstores, distributors and customers with the highest quality books, journals, briefs and publishing execution available anywhere in the world.

CORPORATE PUBLISHING GROUP (CPG)

Establish a Corporate Publishing Program

Turn Your Corporate Information, Research and Analysis Into a New Revenue Stream For Your Company

www.CorporatePublishingGroup.com

Corporate Publishing Group (CPG), the B2B publisher and agent owned by Aspatore, works with leading companies to establish corporate publishing programs, specifically designed to generate a new revenue stream from publishing, build their brand, and reward specific employees with the opportunity to get published. Types of publications published include books, Annual Intelligence Reports, Behind the Business, white papers, newsletters, briefings and journals. Learn how CPG's award winning editors, publicists, marketers and writers can help your business establish a corporate publishing program that can be put in place very quickly, using everyone's time in the most efficient manner possible and help create a new revenue stream from publishing. For more information please e-mail jonp@corporatepublishinggroup.com.

INSIDE THE MINDS

INSIDE THE MINDS: The Real Estate Industry

The Future of Real Estate – Risks, Opportunities, Areas to Watch

Published by Aspatore Books, Inc.
For corrections, company/title updates, comments or any other inquiries please email info@aspatore.com.

First Printing, 2002
10 9 8 7 6 5 4 3 2 1

ISBN 1-58762-064-2

Edited by Jo Alice Hughes, Proofread by Ginger Conlon, Cover design by Kara Yates & Ian Mazie

This book is printed on acid free paper.

A special thanks to all the individuals that made this book possible.

Special thanks to: Ted Juliano, Jeremy Frumkin, Jessica Steiner, Ellen Cunnifee

INSIDE THE MINDS:
The Real Estate Industry
The Future of Real Estate – Risks, Opportunities & Areas to Watch

CONTENTS

CREATING OPPORTUNITIES IN AN EVOLVING INDUSTRY

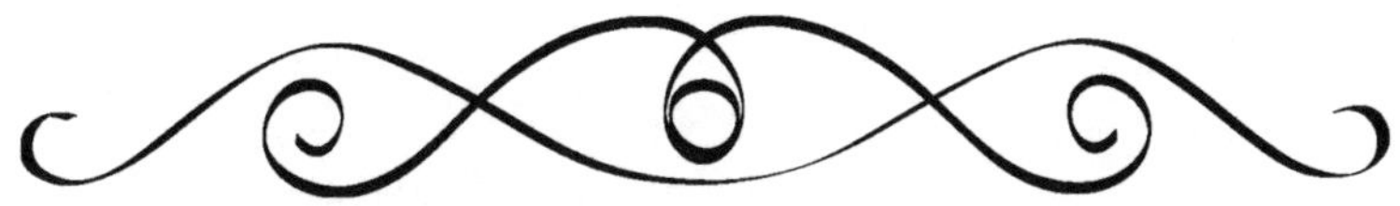

MITCHELL E. HERSH

Mack-Cali Realty Corporation

Chief Executive Officer

Rewards and Challenges

The most exciting aspect of the real estate industry is the opportunities that can be pursued in a variety of ways. Opportunities can be created literally, landscapes changed, and communities revitalized – by the creation of new assets. For example, some of our development opportunities along the Hudson River, in Jersey City, not only serve to provide offices to corporate America but also help to create lifestyle and cultural changes, as well as make a huge impact on a skyline that in the past had been dominated by warehouses. It's gratifying to participate in this evolution and to be able to make a difference in the way people think and look at real estate and architecture and to create economic opportunity for our shareholders. The literal creation of real estate holds a very special place in my thinking and my goals, as does satisfying the needs of corporate America.

One of the most difficult challenges we face is to regain confidence in the economy. Our biggest challenge in real estate is to see the restoration of demand in all sectors.

Until that happens, the real estate industry will be under pressure.

The Evolving Real Estate Industry

The restructuring of public real estate is a very interesting evolution that's been taking place for 35 years. It first emerged in the public sector as mortgage REITs (real estate investment trusts), and then in the early 1990s began to evolve as equity with ownership of hard assets in all sectors: residential, office, retail, and so on. The structure was established under which the income that these public companies generated was in large measure paid back to the investors in the form of dividends. Now the tax legislation is such that REITs are required to pay out 90 percent of their taxable income to shareholders in the form of dividends. REITs are not taxed at the corporate level because income is paid out to individual shareholders, both institutional and retail, in the form of dividends.

REITs have proved to be efficient methods for private real estate owners who need to deal with generational and estate issues. For example, many families contributed their real estate assets to the public company in exchange for what is called an UPREIT (umbrella partnership REIT) share of stock. That is analogous to a common share of stock, but it is held in the UPREIT structure, which basically suspends the property basis, although the UPREIT share has all the attributes. When the holders choose to convert it to a common share of stock, they can do so. The REIT structure offers some unique abilities to deal with matters that pertain to generational issues. That has also helped the industry proliferate.

You have to look at history a bit to understand the efficiencies that have been created in this industry. The public real estate industry has created a high level of information flow, resulting not only from the securitization of the industry, but also from technology and the ability to transmit large volumes of information. That has also created a lot of discipline in capital flows to the real estate industry.

In history's difficult times – for example, in the late 1980s and early 1990s, when we were in a recession – the real estate industry was in disrepair: A lot of capital was flowing to the industry; the banking and thrift industries were deregulated; and savings and loans were in the business of making commercial mortgages. Until the 1986 tax reforms, heavy tax motivation encouraged the building of projects to take advantage of depreciation. If you coupled those two elements, there was a lot of over development in all real estate sectors.

It was easy in those days to finance projects and relatively easy to get approval to build projects in certain parts of the country. This resulted in a huge excess of supply, which, in a bad economy, took a long time to absorb. Now, because of the large amount of available information and because financial institutions can look at real estate stats in any area of the world in terms of supply, demand, vacancy rates, and so on, the capital providers have exercised much greater caution and discipline when providing capital. That has certainly helped maintain a much better balance in supply and demand in the past 10 years or so. The limited availability of land available for development in the northeast corridor and a general limitation on capital have increased discipline. Even though we've been in a tough economy, because there hasn't been overbuilding, the industry will weather the vicissitudes of this economy. We're looking at long-term leases and high-grade credits. We'll get through generally unscathed.

There will always be private and public segments of the industry, but I do think the future will be more efficient. Companies with a lower cost of capital and more access to capital will have greater successes. There will always be niche players, but you will see a trend toward fewer and larger companies that will provide more opportunity for investors and debt holders. Greater efficiency in management teams will be more effective in reducing operating costs. There will be a slightly different shape to the landscape in that relatively small companies will find themselves somewhat limited.

Keys to Success

We are deeply enmeshed in the local fabric of the real estate community. We have to be a well-respected local franchise in all the markets we deal in, and be the landlord of choice, so people think of us when they see an opportunity. Real estate is a local business, and it's also a relationship business. I can't tell you how many times I've run into or gotten a call from someone I haven't seen in years, but who I built a rapport with long ago, and now he or she has a need. Relationships create opportunity. You have to be a part of the community and the real estate community to put yourself in that position.

Another key element is to maintain an extremely flexible balance sheet. Mack-Cali is an investment-grade-rated company, which enables us to access a variety of public capital sources, not only equity capital, but also public debt. We've done a number of debt offerings in the marketplace by virtue of this rating. It also provides investors on both the debt side and the equity side a sense of comfort that the company's balance sheet is managed in a conservative manner, with a high level of coverage on our debt service (so we can provide insulation in terms of our dividend payments). Investors also look at the stability of our income stream and the high credit quality of our tenant base. We know our balance sheet will enable us to quickly take advantage of opportunities.

Taking advantage of opportunity means taking risks. You always look at risk versus reward in any business model, and certainly we try to mitigate risk. When we build new projects, we create risk-adjustment returns that assess the probability of leasing the building. You have to build into an economic model a set of assumptions based on understanding the market and the business. You can protect yourself only to a limited extent, but your projects will tend to perform better if you make reasonable and conservative assumptions. Everything you do in business is evaluating risk adjustment and risk mitigation, and it is all a matter of input quality. The computer can provide answers based only on the information you provide. That takes a clear understanding of the business, and I can't emphasize that enough. It comes from having a feel for the marketplace, as well as the statistics, and having a communications network with corporate America to understand what companies are thinking about in terms of job growth and changing patterns and paradigms. You have to understand industries that affect particular regions where you are considering opportunities.

The best piece of advice I ever received was that the best building is a rented building. Those people who strive for the last straw or the last penny sometimes miss out. If you have a good sense of the marketplace and have the entrepreneurial skills and structure, you'll always be ahead of the curve if you know when to take something off the table. I learned that lesson early in my career, and that's why our company has an occupancy rate that I would hold up to virtually any other in the industry. We keep our buildings full. We know when to take the chips off the table and not to hold out for unrealistic expectations. That lesson is invaluable and is related to the initiative in the company to proactively renew leases in our portfolio. I had a sense that the economic bubble was getting too expansive. I've been in business long enough, as have the members of our board of directors, to understand that the euphoria and unrealistic expectations could not last forever. I told my teams our mission during the period starting about two and a half years ago was to shore up our portfolio. The climate did indeed change, and I think we protected ourselves. This was partially a result of learning early in the game that you should take something off the table and insure yourself against risk. Be entrepreneurial but realistic and conservative in your approach. Understand the risk profile that exists with each opportunity. Recognize what your downside is, and have a reasonable expectation of what your upside will be, given that potential.

To be successful, you need to follow through on the strategic vision and see beyond all the detours in the road. The key is building a strong management team that has the ability to execute the business plan. Also, you need to think about ultimate succession, so there's a continuum of strong management. Maintain flexibility in your balance sheet, so the company is never placed under economic pressure. Manage against risk, so the company is never placed under undue pressure from the volatility of the economy. And think through issues on a long-term basis. Don't react to the attraction *du jour* in the marketplace. Don't overreact to the pressure of Wall Street, but manage your company as a business that you plan to have for a while. Make sure everyone is aligned. You must have alignment between shareholders and debt holders, tenants and employees – in part by creating economic alignments. Your employees are motivated because of their good character and because part of their economic success is tied to the success of the company. All of these things are enmeshed.

The golden rule in real estate, from my perspective, is to have the highest-quality asset base. This means the quality of the bricks and mortar, which depends on the specific location, the general geographic region, the health of the economy, the depth of the infrastructure, accessibility, the kind of tenancy and occupancy, and the reliability of the income stream. Continue to aspire to have the highest-quality asset base possible. This, along with having the best reputation for integrity, will lead the best tenants to want to do business with you.

Mitchell E. Hersh, chief executive officer, director, and member of the Executive Committee of the Board of Directors of Mack-Cali Realty Corporation, is responsible for the company's strategic direction and long-term planning. He is also responsible for creating and implementing Mack-Cali's capital markets strategy and overall investment strategy.

Previously Mr. Hersh held the position of resident and chief operating officer of the company. From 1982 until joining Mack-Cali in December 1997, he served as a partner of The Mack Company and as chief operating officer of The Mack Company since 1990, where he was responsible for overseeing the development, operations, leasing, and acquisitions of The Mack Company's office and industrial portfolio.

SURROGATE SECOND HOMES: THE NEXT STEP IN THE EVOLVING RESORT REAL ESTATE INDUSTRY

ROB MCGRATH

Private Retreats, LLC

President and Chief Executive Officer

Building a Niche for Private Retreats

Having been involved in the resort real estate industry since 1992, first on the finance side on Wall Street and then on the developer side in the Rocky Mountains, I discerned by 1998 that the resort real estate industry was not meeting the needs of a large percentage of consumers. The existing alternatives – second homes, condos, fractional projects, timeshares, rental homes, and hotels – were all missing ingredients that consumers kept asking for. Being focused on the second-home market, I began to look for those missing ingredients.

Other developers had leveraged off the fact that the negatives of owning a second home – the management headaches and large capital commitment required – drove consumers away. The luxury fractional real estate industry was just taking off in the mid-1990s. The product, with its lower price point and lots of services, appeared to answer those two issues. But the sales velocity of those projects was not meeting expectations.

After conducting a couple of surveys in 1998 of around 2,000 consumers who had toured resort real estate projects in the past year but did not buy, I realized the primary reason people do not buy a resort second home is that they do not want to "marry" a single resort. These people did not want to make a long-term commitment to one resort for fear that they would become "bored" with that location.

The results of the surveys confirmed that a "surrogate second home" product with houses in a variety of mountain, beach, and golf locations would appeal to a large demographic group.

Some of the luxury fractional developers had developed properties in more than one location, but the selection of resorts was limited to just two or three locations, and it would be many years before these developers could offer more than just a few locations. A second problem was that even if they could offer a variety of locations in the future, the mechanism for "trading" or "swapping" one location for another was cumbersome and inflexible.

So I set out with three partners to create a product that would allow people to "own" a luxury resort home in 20 or more locations. Our model focused on that identified need of people to own a second home while not having to marry just one resort. And Private Retreats was born. Today, the club is limited to a maximum of 400 members who each have the unlimited right to use up to $60 million worth of resort real estate homes in 26 resorts around the world.

The members use these homes on an unlimited basis – as they would if they actually owned $60 million worth of second homes. As with Net Jets and other fractional jet companies, we have developed a probability model that allows the company to rent houses (or, in the case of fractional jet companies, to charter jets) from approved vendors whenever there is a conflict in a location.

In addition to the real estate itself, the club has specifically been developed as a "lifestyle" product. Numerous unique amenities and benefits that are not practically replicable by an individual, are delivered to the members free of charge, or at dramatically reduced costs.

This "lifestyle" aspect of the club is very important because we believe we do not actually sell resort real estate. What we sell is a "lifestyle." It's why our logo is, "Private Retreats: The Art of Living Well." The real estate the club owns is a means to an end, that end being our members' ultimate enjoyment of their family, friends, and free time.

These amenities and benefits include a full-time service staff – from a personal concierge staff (experts on the "ins and outs" of these resorts) who plan all the members' trips, to a host to pick them up when they arrive and drop them off at the house. Before they arrive, the concierge staff has booked their balloon ride and dinner reservations and made sure their tee-times and spa appointments are set, and the host has already put their groceries in the home and confirmed that their private chef is coming in every morning.

In addition to the personal staff, they have a Porsche, BMW, or Mercedes in their garage when they arrive. Members regularly fly in on one of the club's private prop-planes or jets for costs that are often competitive with commercial air rates. Every member has access to the local private spa, golf, and skiing.

The fee to join the club is currently $185,000 and rising. If the member decides to leave the club, the fee is refunded. Members pay annual dues of $6,850 to cover the overhead to operate all the real estate, and a $150-per-day fixed fee for the house itself (regardless of the number of people who stay there), which gives the member access to the amenities described earlier. In the beach resorts, the houses usually stand on their own lots, have three or four bedrooms, and often have a pool, a hot tub, and a view. In the mountains, the houses are typically luxury townhouses or penthouse condominiums that are slopeside.

We look for a number of qualities in our locations:

- ❑ The resort must have a brand name. Telluride is well known; Paskapoo, near Calgary, Alberta, is not.
- ❑ The resort town must have access to world-class golf or skiing and offer a variety of activities in addition.
- ❑ At beach resorts, the club prefers to have the house no more than 200 yards from the beach (being directly on

the beach is often not financially feasible, given the price of the membership) and right on the golf course. In mountain resorts the club seeks slopeside houses.

- The houses must be new or no older than two or three years.

Private Retreats is a thriving company with a now proven market niche that we believe will only grow in the future.

Leading a Real Estate Company

To build and lead a company from nothing to $20 million–plus in revenue per year, you need to have personal skill sets in a variety of areas. You have to understand and execute across the board. Rather than discuss a series of rules or processes you must master to be such a leader, here are some things I've found useful over the past several years.

Our business has four main divisions:

Sales & Marketing: For the first two years of the company, I was its primary salesperson. I firmly believe if you do not know how to sell your own product, you will never build a successful company from the ground up. This may be the most important lesson I learned in building Private Retreats: If the founder cannot sell the product, no one can.

With marketing, my number one rule is, "Try, try again." The first 30 ideas you try are likely to be duds. Or you may have one or two good, workable ideas in them, but the process you employ is flawed.

My number two rule: An unproven marketing program should cost little or no money to implement the first time or two. Do not spend money on people or products until they prove they can effectively and efficiently deliver prospects to you. You are taking a big risk with your time (and some money). They must bear some of the risk, as well. If they are not willing to bear some of the risk by being paid for performance and not up-front, then look elsewhere for help. Companies can easily go broke allowing "experts" to run up big marketing bills on unproven ideas. Remember, no one knows your product as well as you do. Don't be fooled that some "expert" knows better than you. They don't.

Regardless, you need only one or two methods that consistently work to find enough prospects to build your business. Your goal needs to be to find those one or two great methodologies that can consistently deliver prospects to you.

Development/Acquisitions: I have never had to become technically competent in building these buildings, but I have had to become generally aware of the processes involved so I could keep costs in line. For the acquisitions team, I look for people who have been in the market for at least 10 years and know what to look for and how to negotiate and close a real estate transaction.

Hospitality: Taking care of the people who have put their trust in you must be the company's number one priority after sales. Once someone has decided to buy your product, you must deliver unconditionally, even if doing so sometimes costs you money. If you deliver unconditionally, you will eventually succeed because most companies don't.

Here's an analogy: You go to a local restaurant and find a bug in your soup (or the tuna is overcooked or the wine is bad). Most restaurants will say they are sorry, take the soup back, and either offer you another bowl (which I doubt you will want, since the whole batch is probably tainted), or they'll not charge you for the soup. Now, does that give you a reason to come back to that restaurant? Absolutely not. What did they just do for you? First, they inconvenienced you. Second, they made you uncomfortable (Is all the food here tainted?). Third, they did not charge you for the inconvenience they caused you. I suggest a different approach. We'd offer, *of course,* not to charge you for the soup, and ask if you would like one of our specialty salads, on the house. With food costs of maybe 25 percent, this might cost the restaurant $2.00, but it has just increased the chances of a return customer by 1000 percent. And, since the free salad is such a unique occurrence in the restaurant industry, it's likely you'll mention the pleasant surprise you had at our restaurant to your friends tomorrow.

For the Hospitality division I look for trained general management types with long-term, five-star hotel experience. We try to deliver the kinds of services and personal attention that are delivered only in the best hotels, so the people who have been doing that for a long time are the ones best qualified for the job.

Finance: More than anything else, managing the money is the key to success. You must solidly understand the relationships between cash flows and have a core understanding of the economic risks you take and don't take.

Finally, I like to run the company so each manager has full and complete accountability for what he or she is supposed to deliver. A primary tool we use is weekly workshop meetings. While the processes and regular implementation have already been set up, incremental improvement is the key to our success today. A typical workshop meeting in Hospitality might begin when the head of Hospitality asks the staff to recount the top two issues facing them in their jobs today. The group then selects an issue or two for which a solution should be sought. They then ask each staff member to come up with their two best ideas for solving the problem. Over 52 weeks each division comes up with 52 great ideas to solve its own problems. This has allowed us to improve processes without a lot of change at the corporate level.

Marketing Resort Memberships

Keys to marketing any product are to differentiate, to limit supply, and to identify and create a structured sales process that focuses on creating a number of direct and unique contacts with the prospect. People want unique products that are hard to get, and they want to be given a fun, easy-to-follow road map for becoming educated enough about the product to make an intelligent decision.

It took our company a year to figure out how to effectively differentiate our product from the competition, another year to figure out how to limit the available supply, and a third year to figure out how to make it easy and fun for the prospect to become educated about our product. When the third piece fell into place, the company's sales volume exploded.

First, our product is characterized by three points of differentiation:

1. We offer unlimited use of our houses, while the competition has placed limits on its customers.
2. We offer more than 20 locations, while the competition offers three at the most.
3. We offer packages of amenities, benefits, and personal service that are absolutely unmatched in the industry.

It took a lot of work and thought to create those three differentiating points, but they are the basis on which we built the company.

Second, to provide unlimited use to our members, we always knew we had to have a geographically diversified pool of members. If all the members lived in the same place, they would have similar travel patterns, and certain locations would be overrun with requests, while others would sit empty. To diversify our member base, we divided the country into 35 geographic markets with no more than 12 to 15 memberships available in any one market. For example, in Chicago we had 15 memberships available. This means that once 15 people from Chicago joined Private Retreats, there were no more memberships available in that market. With that small number of memberships available, we entered the market by telling our friends and acquaintances and a short list of people who had previously shown an interest in buying a resort second home that we were now offering memberships in Chicago (they were previously not available in Chicago). We then set up personal appointments in Chicago with each interested party to talk more in-depth about who we are. We met about 30 people, and of that group, 15 individuals signed a reservation agreement that allowed them a 45-day "free look" at the club. They each put up a $5,000 reservation deposit to gain that right.

Third, when these 15 individuals had signed a reservation agreement, they were introduced to an educational process that follows several steps designed to fully explain all the information about the club. That process is fun and interesting for the prospect and ultimately created 12 new Private Retreats members.

The Future of the Industry

In a fragmenting world, by definition consumer offerings will become more diverse. However, most of the real estate industry is not working toward this. In general, the resort real estate industry is about five to 10 years behind the curve. The Baby Boom generation is a huge market for the real estate industry, and their demands for new and unique offerings will only increase over the next several years. But one thing is clear: Different people need different types of offerings, and the real estate resort industry will find ways to deliver them.

Quite a few smart people are focused on new ways to deliver resort real estate to the consumer, and a few of them will succeed. Fragmentation in the industry will continue, and new product types will come out and follow in our footsteps or others. Other real estate developers will use our business model and others to satisfy the wants and needs of the high-end and mid-level resort traveler who wants a second home.

Private Retreats itself will expand to meet these needs. Our business model is highly scalable into different niches, and we are already developing the new products we will offer over the next few years.

Rob McGrath has been president and CEO of Private Retreats, LLC since 1998. Before Private Retreats he was involved in a number of resort real estate developments in the western United States. As a commercial mortgage-backed securities trader at J.P. Morgan and Nomura Securities, he financed several billion dollars' worth of real estate loans. Before Wall Street Mr. McGrath was an award-winning professional ski racer on the World Pro Ski Tour.

Mr. McGrath graduated with honors from Dartmouth College in 1982. At Dartmouth he majored in comparative mythology and was Captain of the Dartmouth Ski Team. He earned an MBA in finance from the Tuck School of Business at Dartmouth in 1991 as one of only 15 Tuck Scholars.

MEETING THE CHALLENGES OF CHANGE IN THE REAL ESTATE INDUSTRY

MICHAEL J. ALTER

The Alter Group

President

The Move From Main Street to Wall Street

Real estate has historically been a ma-and-pa business. Through the housing boom of the 1950s, the rise of retail malls and hotels in the 1960s, and the slate of trophy properties in the 1970s and 1980s, real estate stayed in the hands of industrious individuals who ended up making profound changes to the way we work and live. The complexion of real estate changed significantly only during the 1990s. As pension funds, insurance companies, and private financiers retrenched after the crash of the early 1990s, Wall Street seized the moment and went into an acquisition frenzy through vulture funds, REITs (real estate investment trusts), and the emergent commercial mortgage-backed securities (CMBS) market, which helped lift the industry out of its recession. The government played a big part in this through the establishment of the Resolution Trust Corporation (RTC), which put about $456 billion of assets belonging to failed S&Ls (savings and loan institutions) on the market. This enormous transfer of property changed the industry overnight. In 10 years, between 1990 and 2000, the number of REITs alone doubled. CMBS issuance grew from $4.8 million to $44 billion between 1990 and 1997.

Real estate has many independent components that are affected overall by finance and the capital markets. The securitization with collateralized loans and the advent of public money into the industry have had a huge impact, generating a new source of liquidity and an accompanying level of discipline. That's not to say it was an easy transition. In 1998 thin spreads in the CMBS markets and over-building and over-acquisition by the REITs were met with plunging values. In response, the market was chastened. REITs have changed over the past 10 years from growth companies to utility companies with dividends and remain good return vehicles.

The securitization of the real estate industry and the emergence of REITs have caused companies to be run much more professionally: "More Wall Street and less Main Street" was the catchphrase of the mid-1990s. Only a few family-owned companies were able to survive in this new higher-stakes world, but the ones that did grew stronger and have acquired national and even international prominence.

Technology, of course, continues to have a large impact on the industry. Furthermore, the public markets drove an increasing reliance on sophisticated research to protect their investment. Information is now available very quickly. Companies such as CoStar Group and Property & Portfolio Research Information (PPR) track billions of square feet of real estate. All the major brokerage houses also issue periodic market surveys. In the early days real estate was a local game. If you did not already know the market and its players, you were hard-pressed to succeed.

Gradually we will see technology change how we do business – from how deals are transacted to how buildings are designed and built. While construction is still very paper-intensive, eventually you will see critical functions done through intranets and the Internet. According to Forrester Research, the amount of business transacted via the Web in the world construction industry will reach $141 billion, or 11 percent, by 2004. Why should a construction company adopt Web-based project management applications? Because inefficiencies and delays account for $200 billion of the $650 billion spent on construction in America. To illustrate, using sophisticated platforms like Bidcom, Cephren, or Buzzsaw, a developer on a $40,000,000 building can save as much as 5 percent in the project's costs, yielding a savings of as much as $2,000,000 in rent over a 10-year term.

Many have also theorized that the increasing sophistication of real estate technology will somehow make the broker superfluous, or vastly diminished in importance. I actually think it has done the opposite: It has enhanced the level of professionalism within the community because today's broker is more informed, more cognizant of all the issues pertaining to development, and generally able to add more value to the process. In the end, reams of research and numbers can never take the place of a seasoned broker in representing the interests of clients.

I am pleased the industry has learned from what happened in the go-go 1980s and 1990s. We have done a better job of managing our growth to be able to survive the current downturn in relatively good shape. The current overhang of sublease space in the market is a concern, but we should see that whittle down during the next 12 months, with vacancies coming down to the low double digits across the country. This makes me optimistic going forward. It shows a real maturity on the part of the industry.

On the slightly more negative side, I still think real estate has not received the attention it deserves within big companies. It is still treated somewhat as a non-core business. We saw that change a little in the 1990s, but it is still surprising to me that companies, despite the commitment of significant resources in real estate, do not focus enough attention at the board level to their assets.

Succeeding in a Changing Market

The most challenging aspect of the industry is what makes it most fun – there is never a dull moment. It is multidisciplinary – you deal with finance, construction, and design. You work with demographic trends, supply chain issues, municipal growth patterns, quality of life concerns. It is also a deal-driven business. Things are constantly moving; there is never not something happening.

To succeed in this changing market, you must be flexible, entrepreneurial, opportunistic, and able to move quickly. When you see something happening, you have to react to it immediately. You drive past a site and see nothing but dirt and then drive by a year later and see a building in that spot. Why? Because someone saw something there that you didn't. The trick is to make sure you see it first.

In this industry you have to have an appetite for risk. Deciding the right risks is the whole ballgame. To manage risk you must have a realistic assessment of the upside, but you have to measure the downside, too. As a wise investor, always diversify: You might take a greater risk with fewer resources committed to it because if you end up on the losing end, you will have a sustainable loss.

To lead a real estate organization, you have to be a generalist, know what you do not know, and take in the big picture. My philosophy has been to find talented people and stay out of their way. I provide the direction and make the decisions that need to be made, but let them do what they do well. I do not micromanage.

In terms of management, we try to be hierarchically flat. This allows us to provide the highest level of service to our customers because they know they are only a phone call away from the ultimate decision-maker. Eschewing layers of bureaucracy within our company also creates freedom in the organization. If someone has an idea, they do not hesitate to bring it up. We make sure good ideas are rewarded. We are also a very client-driven organization. Our sales mission is not only to sell but to listen – to anticipate client needs. This is an imperative that is continually driven into the company culture – through sales meetings, reviews, and companywide briefings. You must have the right people, and they need to know what they should be looking for to have this work.

Personally, I make sure I leave myself enough time to interact with peers, lenders, investors, and so on. I try to talk to other business leaders to learn their perspectives. I don't want to get tunnel vision and lose sight of what's going on at the macroeconomic level, so I force myself to get out there and see what's happening. I am also a voracious reader; reading is a source of improvement and inspiration to me, and I try to listen and learn from others.

Life Cycle of a Real Estate Deal

The first step in a real estate deal is finding the opportunity – for example, an opportunity to develop a speculative office building. After the crash of the 1990s there was no money available for new real estate development, so we thought it would be a great time to build spec office property because few of our competitors could get the financing. The Alter Group was fortunate in that we had very strong financials, lines of credit with a network of lenders, and a sizable portfolio that was more than 90 percent leased. We anticipated that building spec office property was a smart move because, as the economy improved, office demand would pick up.

Second, figure out what cities you need to be in. Often a niche market like Dulles, Virginia, or Lombard, Illinois, might have good fundamentals in place and allow you to have a long-term presence. In many cases clients take you to markets where they have to be. The Alter Group has developed during the past 12 months in Temple, Texas; Bremerton, Washington; and Independence, Kentucky.

Once you've arrived, figure out who else is there, what kind of growth there will be, what other opportunities there are, and how to position yourself within that sub-market.

Fourth, find a particular site and the right entitlement process. Fifth, define the product itself – if it's office, what kind of a building (high-rise, mid-rise, single-story, etc.) you'll develop. Sixth, find the financing for the project. And finally, sell the product.

Real Estate Advice

When asked for advice on how to succeed in the real estate industry, I tell people the following:

1. Do not let your ego get in the way.
2. Keep an eye on the big picture and the overall vision. Keep attuned the markets of the world. We are a global economy. In 1998 a crisis in the Russian debt markets dislocated the U.S. CMBS market, with enormous repercussions for the industry.
3. Be decisive. Do not be afraid to take risks. When opportunities come, you must decide quickly whether or not to take them.
4. Manage the people and maintain the culture. Keep people focused and happy.
5. Building relationships is what it's all about. People have to trust you. So do what you say you will do; that's what credibility is based on. And don't forget to listen to and understand the customer.

As president, Michael J. Alter is responsible for all planning and operations of The Alter Group, a national corporate real estate development firm with five vertically integrated companies. Affiliates include Alter+Care, a healthcare real estate development firm; Alter Construction Company and Alter Design Builders, which provide construction services; and Alter Asset Management, a property-management firm. Additionally, Mr. Alter is managing director of Ground Zero, a joint venture with Sterling Capital, Ltd., that develops telco hotels (buildings or parts of buildings housing functioning telecommunications equipment) and data centers.

A Chicago native, Mr. Alter previously was a practicing attorney with Mayer Brown & Platt and a clerk to William J. Bauer, former Chief Judge of the Seventh Circuit U.S. Court of Appeals.

Mr. Alter established and is president of City Year Chicago, now in its seventh year. This unique national service organization unites young people from diverse backgrounds, ages 17 to 23, for a demanding year of full-time community service and leadership development.

Mr. Alter has a BA degree in government from Harvard University and a JD degree from the University of Chicago. He is a licensed attorney in Illinois and has an honorary degree from Knox College.

TECHNOLOGY & THE MODERN REIT: A REVOLUTION IN THE OFFICE PLACE

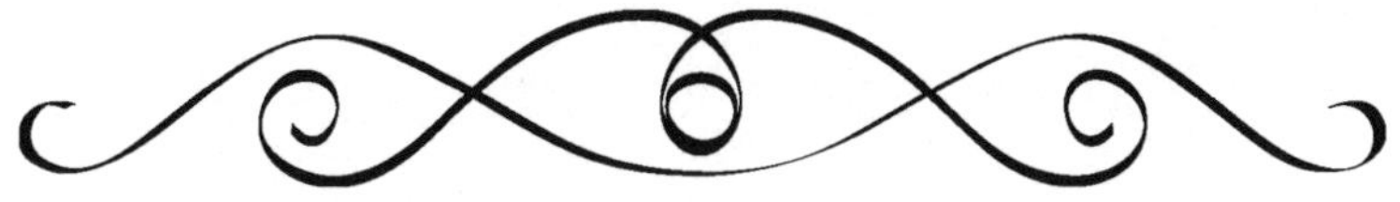

WILLIAM T. ATKINS

AmeriVest Properties Inc.

Chairman and Chief Executive Officer

Bigger – But Not Necessarily Better

When you were a child, did you ever play the game, "What's wrong with this picture?" That's the one where a picture looks normal at first glance, but on closer examination, you see little things out of place. The lampshade is upside down; a man is wearing only one shoe; and so on. When I look at the way we perceive the U.S. economy, it occurs to me that there is something wrong with the picture.

"Big, not best," has always been the American calling card. In fact, I bet you can't drive more than 75 miles in any direction, from anywhere in the U.S., without running into a "biggest in the world" of some sort. Listen to the chatter when the Fortune 500 comes out. Few chiefs comment on their profit or return on assets. The question is, "What's your rank?" "Making the Fortune 500 – an attribute based on size alone – is the Holy Grail for most non-members; moving up is the Holy Grail for most members," as Tom Peters began his 1987 book *Thriving on Chaos.* America has always believed bigger is better. To assess how the country is doing, both individual and institutional investors are preoccupied with the Dow Jones Industrial Average, the S&P 500 average, or the NASDAQ. Each of these measures only the largest corporations in America. Congress focuses far more hours deliberating how to help large companies in steel, autos, energy, and manufacturing cope with foreign competition than it spends on policies that will strengthen the competitive position of small business. Turn to the business section of your local newspaper: Large national companies capture the vast majority of copy, and coverage of local companies is limited to only the largest ones. We still live by the 1920s maxim: "What's good for General Motors is good for America."

It's time to wake up. What's wrong with this picture? For the past 50 years, most, if not all, of America's economic and job growth has come from small businesses. In his landmark study, "Job Creation in America," David Birch asserts that more than 100 percent of the country's net new jobs are created by firms with fewer than 100 employees. The U.S. Bureau of Statistics reports that during the 1990s

75 percent of the country's net new jobs were created by small businesses – and, important for real estate, these small businesses were responsible for 90 percent of the growth in business-space demand. "Bigness has not delivered the goods," say Walter Adams and James W. Brock, in their book *The Bigness Complex.* They go on to add, "Scientific evidence has not been kind to the apostles of bigness and to their mythology." As early as 1986 *U.S. News & World Report* attributed the continued economic success of Los Angeles – perhaps the most successful economic region in the country – to the fact that "some 90 percent of those employed in the area work in small firms with fewer than 50 people." Small firms are also more innovative. According to Adams and Brock, a National Science Board study reveals, "The smallest firms produced about four times as many innovations per R&D dollar as the middle sized firms and twenty-four times as many as the largest firms." Small, entrepreneurial firms are driving the U.S. economy.

Our nation's small businesses are the unsung heroes and the backbone of our economic prosperity, and they now employ about half the people working in this country. Yet these businesses receive little of the credit for the strength of our economy and the resultant well-being of our people.

The "bigger is better" syndrome also applies to commercial real estate. When you think of the best office buildings in the country, huge complexes housing extremely large corporations come to mind: Rockefeller Center and Citicorp Center in New York, the Embarcadero Center in San Francisco, Enron Tower and the Galleria in Houston… the list goes on. When terrorists chose to attack the symbol of American greatness, they targeted the World Trade Center in New York. These properties represent American business – big business. The vast majority of institutional real estate investors vie for trophy properties with large-credit tenants on long-term leases. They believe these properties represent a better long-term investment. Time and again they have been proved wrong. Enron, Arthur Andersen, Global Crossing, K-Mart … all grab headlines for their spectacular falls only months after reports of high "credit quality." Most of the focus and finances of investors are on large-tenant properties, while small businesses are relegated to B- and C-class properties. You need only look as far as the average tenant sizes in publicly held office investment companies. Corporate Office Properties Trust – 17,000 square feet; Equity Office Properties Trust – 12,500 square feet. Yet the average small business occupies between 2,000 and 4,000 square feet. It is obvious that in the office investment world, bigger is still better.

Big Change on the Horizon

But the foundation for a radically different office market is in place. Four converging trends promise to alter the way offices of the future are owned and managed.

First, the office sector has become increasingly important within the commercial real estate industry. In 1900 the most important sectors of commercial real estate were farms and factories. As the economy has made the transition from agriculture- and manufacturing- to service-based, the demand for and importance of offices have grown. In 1900 only about 25 percent of the workers in

America were employed by service businesses. Today the number is about 75 percent. Today more than half the working population is housed in offices, and this trend will continue. Because of the high standard of living and resultant demand for a higher quality of life both financially and environmentally, workers will increasingly prefer office environments.

The second trend is the transition from large to small businesses. As large companies have downsized and outsourced, the percentage of office space occupied by small businesses has more than doubled, now accounting for more than half the office space in the U.S. Because of the competitiveness of world markets and the impact of technology, business cycles have greatly accelerated. The pace of change has rapidly increased, making it harder for large companies to sustain any competitive advantage. Smaller, more nimble and innovative firms will increase market share and continue to increase their relative share of the economy.

The third trend is the rapid developments in technology during the past 25 years, especially those enabled by the development of low-cost personal computers. This has made small companies more productive and allowed for a broader base of office users outside of corporate headquarters.

Finally, the emergence of the modern Real Estate Investment Trust (REIT) during the 1990s has permanently altered the dynamics of real estate ownership. A new publicly-held corporate owner of real estate has emerged as a long-term owner in the office sector.

Much has been written on the first two trends – small businesses and a service economy. Now let's focus on the latter two: technology and the modern REITs.

Emerging Technology

The explosion of technology in the last quarter of the 20th century is having a profound impact on small businesses, and therefore, the office sector. Office buildings of the 1980s were really not much different from those of the 1920s. They were taller, had faster elevators, and had computerized systems running their heating and air conditioning systems. But buildings were primarily "bricks and mortar." The only way to distinguish a building was by its architectural style. Large corporations continued to occupy increasingly modern edifices, but once inside, these buildings all looked and functioned pretty much the same. These large businesses were able to keep up with technology themselves and did not need the building owner's help to do so.

Enter the age of small business. Technological advances, coupled with cost efficiencies created a huge demand by small companies for high-speed computer connections and all the ancillary services stemming from computerization. Fiber connections and distribution, interoffice LANs, video conferencing, computer-driven security systems, and presentation technology are just a few of the advancements small businesses need but are unable to afford on their own. A few responsive office owners are beginning to provide these amenities on a shared basis to small tenants in their buildings. Technology will truly become the granite of this century. Building owners will have to take the lead in providing the latest technology to their small business tenants because, unlike their former large tenants, these businesses cannot afford to acquire this technology themselves. In 1999 a Building Owners & Managers Association survey of office tenants nationwide found the five factors most important to the tenants were all technology-based. Interestingly, more than 50 percent were in buildings that had *none* of the five.

A new mindset will be required. Institutions have traditionally looked at tenants as a necessary evil of owning office buildings. They have preferred large credit-worthy tenants on long leases because they represented less trouble. Small tenants require shorter leases and more service. It is not an accident that institutions view industrial warehouses as the best investment class – these require almost no management. Continuing this mentality in the office environment is a formula for failure. As institutions fight over the decreasing space demands of large Fortune

500 companies, returns will fall. As the leasing environment becomes more and more competitive, building amenities and customer service will become the key differentiating factors in office space decisions. Innovative office space owners who embrace the needs of smaller businesses and provide the work environment they require will earn the profits.

The Modern REIT

In 1960 Congress enacted the law creating Real Estate Investment Trusts, patterned after the mutual fund laws enacted in 1936. Simply put, the law was intended to enable individual investors access to commercial real estate investments that previously been available only to institutions and very wealthy individuals. In theory, by allowing publicly traded REITs to invest in income-producing real estate and be exempt from corporate taxes (as long as they paid out most of their profits in dividends), individuals who owned their stock would be on an equal basis with institutional investors who owned the real estate directly. Thus ownership of hotels, office buildings, and apartment buildings – or at least parts of these – would be possible for the individual investor. In the early years REITs became very popular and evolved into a source of capital for the entrepreneurs of the real estate industry.

Before REITs became available as a source of capital, most real estate entrepreneurs had relied on high leverage in the form of bank or insurance company loans to enable them to participate in the industry. Only large institutions or extremely wealthy individuals could build an office building or apartment complex without borrowing money. Unfortunately, as these entrepreneurs began to take advantage of the capital available through public REITs, they continued to borrow as they had before – except that now the equity capital was no longer theirs or from a sophisticated institutional investor. It was relatively unsophisticated public money. In the past the optimism of real estate entrepreneurs had been tempered by the availability of capital. Now capital was readily available, and the optimism continued unbridled.

The result was tragic. REITs became over-leveraged in a very cyclical business, and the inevitable happened. Most of the individual investors Congress had intended to help by opening the door to commercial real estate investing lost money – lots of it. Real estate developed a reputation as a risky business run by out-of-control deal junkies who would take unwise risks with the public's investments. The enactment of the 1986 tax reform acts and the savings and loan scandals of the late 1980s did nothing to improve this image, and ultimately led to a crash in commercial real estate values that sealed the fate of all but the very best run and low-leveraged REITs.

Out of this rubble, the modern REIT was born in the early 1990s. Using far less leverage and run by professional "corporate" management, these REITs began to attract both individual and institutional investment. Individuals liked the returns and dividends, and institutions liked the ability to balance their portfolios by buying or selling daily – something not possible if you own the real estate directly. Also, following the spectacular fall of limited partnerships in the 1980s, both welcomed the transparency and liquidity required of a public company. During the 1990s investments in publicly traded REITs increased from less than $10 billion to more than $150 billion, and the modern REIT firmly established itself as the investment vehicle of choice for income-producing real estate. Finally, the Congressional vision of the 1960s had become a reality.

In the future the trend will continue, and traded public investment companies will own more and more of America's commercial real estate. As this happens, these companies will become increasingly specialized. We're already seeing golf course REITs, prison REITs, self-storage REITs, health care REITs, timber REITs, and REITs specializing in sale leasebacks of real estate to automotive dealers, movie theaters, and restaurants. Management firms will become experts in various segments of income properties, and increasingly the performance gap between knowledgeable management with a specific focus and others with a more generalized approach will widen. Public markets have historically rewarded superior performance and will do so with REITs. Higher stock valuations mean lower capital costs, and real estate is a capital-intensive industry. The superior managed companies will dominate the industry.

The Service Revolution

It is worth noting a fifth trend that will soon come into play in the office industry: the service revolution. During the 1980s Tom Peters and others documented the success of companies that brought a service mentality to their respective industries. At that time the U.S. economy was faltering, and many attribute the resurgence of America to companies embracing customer service as a fundamental of their businesses. However, few small tenants would ever use the words "service" and "landlord" in the same sentence. Smart building owners who recognize that their business is no longer just "bricks and mortar," to be passively leased and managed, but rather a work environment designed to increase the productivity of their small tenant-partners, will be justly rewarded. Those who don't recognize this transformation will fall behind.

Real estate executives have been willing to make large investments and reap the rewards over a long period. Technology requires that they make large investments that could become obsolete in only a few years. The entire risk-reward life cycle of the industry is changing. Managements will have to be much quicker and much smarter. Their customers are demanding it, and their competitors are adapting. A "beautiful" building is no longer enough. It's what's inside that counts – and what matters to a new generation of tenants.

Office Real Estate Sector Today: Risks and Rewards

Rapid change always creates risks and opportunities. The office real estate sector today faces several obvious ones.

"Location, location, location" has always been the golden rule of real estate investing. Obviously, with the technology available to smaller and smaller companies, location can be almost anywhere. Video conferencing and computer communication are here today and, some say, threaten the need for office space at all. Although I do not subscribe to that theory, the implications for the work place are still significant. People will no longer need or desire to work in highly centralized, congested locations; yet completely embracing the virtual office means giving up the creative synergy of face-to-face and chance encounters. It is no longer necessary or desirable to have all employees in a single location. Instead, future offices will be in smaller groupings located conveniently to those employees. As the "bigger is better" myth fades, the desirability of offices in a huge "trophy" property in a congested downtown center may fade. Synergistic divisions will locate in the area most convenient to their employees and be connected by technology to other groups. Even large companies will create smaller and smaller office groupings as buildings provide infrastructure to enable them to do so, and their employees demand it. There are enormous implications to both centralized metropolitan areas and suburban land planning from these trends.

This trend has already started with the biggest employer of all, the federal government. Since the Oklahoma City bombing, the federal government has been splitting up divisions, relocating entire departments, spreading employees into more and more buildings in various areas. The safety concerns regarding employee concentration and access will continue to drive government and large corporations to smaller and smaller offices, further complicating the lives of large-tenant office-building owners. The "one size fits all employees" approach to leasing will no longer work.

Lenders will also have to adapt to this new reality. Traditionally, loans have driven growth in the office sector – whether from banks, insurance companies, or Wall Street. The risks to these lenders are increasing dramatically. For the industry, this probably means lower loan-to-value ratios and a requirement for more seasoned management experience and stronger balance sheets. This will further support the trend to publicly traded REITs. For the lenders, management will become an increasingly important component. While they have historically relied on the property and location to secure their investment, in the future this will no longer be enough. Management's ability to adapt to changing physical requirements and technology will underscore the safety of their loans. Real estate is becoming corporate and, therefore, subject to the same changes in their customers' demands as other industries.

For small businesses there is nothing but good news on the horizon. No longer will they receive the leftovers of the office market. Offices in the future will provide environments designed to enhance small business productivity. Technology features and amenities will be built into the offices of the future. Small companies will be able to focus on their business, and their office landlord-partners will help them become more efficient, more productive, and more profitable. By leveraging the resources of the landlord and a new generation of office space, the small companies of the new millennium will continue to prosper and grow – driving the economy forward in this decade and beyond.

The trend is unmistakable. The age of the elephant is past. We have entered the age of the gazelle.

William T. Atkins is the chairman and chief executive officer of AmeriVest Properties Inc., a real estate investment trust listed on the American Stock Exchange. In its five years as a public company, AmeriVest has grown revenues in excess of 50 percent per year and has delivered average annual total returns to its shareholders of 24 percent. Both performances are near the top in the real estate industry and lead the office sector.

Before joining AmeriVest, Mr. Atkins was the president of E. K. Williams & Co., an international consulting and accounting firm serving small businesses. He also cofounded and was a senior executive of Watkins Pacific Corporation, a multinational, publicly traded conglomerate now based in Brisbane, Australia.

In 1971 Mr. Atkins received his Bachelor of Arts degree from Stanford University in economics. Mr. Atkins currently resides in Denver and Santa Barbara.

SUCCEEDING IN REAL ESTATE INVESTMENT

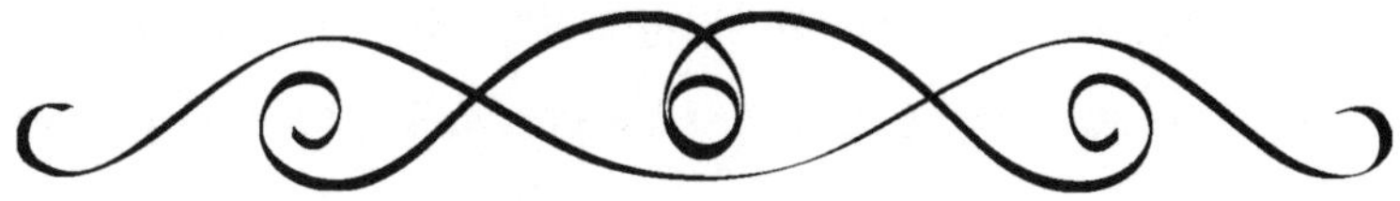

JOHN C. GOFF

Crescent Real Estate Equities Company

Vice-Chairman and Chief Executive Officer

Check the *Front* Page for the Big Picture

To successfully lead a real estate investment company, it is critical to be able to see the "big picture" – not only identifying major trends in the real estate industry itself but, even more important, identifying trends and changes not directly related to real estate that will have an impact on the demand for space and the financial health of the users. This may include having a view of the national economy, along with the regional economies in which you're invested. Demographic changes also are very important to understand and track, as they have profound longer-term impact on the demand for space. Is there a trend of the talented labor pool migrating to certain locations within our borders? If so, why? Where are companies relocating? Why? Will these trends continue?

The strategy for which I built Crescent was founded on a thorough understanding of these trends – principally, the ongoing population shift from the Northeast to the Southwestern U.S. This shift has created a significant talent pool in the Southwest that is very attractive to companies, causing them to relocate and expand within certain Southwestern U.S. markets. The best investment ideas come from the front page of the newspaper as opposed to the business section. Look for the big trends.

In addition to seeing the big picture, a leader must be energetic and focused and must be a team builder. It is important to be a good listener, soliciting opinions, questions and feedback, whether positive or negative. I tend to provide the strategic direction and surround myself with real pros to execute that strategy. I make sure the team has appropriate incentives, that they stay on track, and that the strategy is constantly reevaluated based on changes in the economy, the marketplace in which we operate, and other "big picture" impacts. While in essence being a "cheerleader" much of the time, a leader must also be able to synthesize a lot of ideas, details, and thoughts into clear, simple communication.

Assembling the team to execute the strategy is vital in the real estate business, as in any business. The unique challenge in real estate is that it is inherently an entrepreneurial or "deal" business, as well as an operational business. Every acquisition and every lease is a "deal" requiring transactional expertise that is entrepreneurial in nature. Property management and financial reporting require operational expertise with high attention to detail and the ability to deal with a large number of very important customers. About 70,000 customers reside in our properties every day. A property manager must take ownership of his or her building and customers, which requires a unique skill set. These property managers must have the ability to make immediate decisions to respond to the needs of their customers without dealing with a corporate-level bureaucracy.

Additionally, the business is becoming much more sophisticated and disciplined because of the source of capital now driving the industry. The sophistication of Wall Street, pension funds, and large banks that now dominate the capital flowing into real estate requires that we be more "institutionalized" in the way we manage and report on our business. This presents a challenge for the CEO. I spend a great deal of time blending the talent, the incentives, the infrastructure, and the controls required to keep the team energized and executing our strategy, while at the same time meeting the requirements of our capital partners. This is a new challenge for our industry created by its recapitalization over the past 10 years.

Plan to Succeed

We have made a sizable investment in financial reporting systems that are fully integrated with our operating systems. We constantly measure our progress against our plan, thoroughly reviewing reports, many of which are available on a real-time basis, as well as a monthly package that goes through an extensive review. This data tells us whether we are meeting our targets, and it provides early warning if we are not, so we can take corrective action quickly. We have incentives for the full management team, based on both their individual performance and the overall profitability of the company. Properly aligned incentives are as important as the strategy itself.

Our incentive plan is structured to provide three targets:

1. Company profitability (highly quantifiable)
2. Property-specific or department-specific goals (highly quantifiable)
3. Individual goals (more subjective)

Each manager has a weighting assigned to each category based on their particular function. For example, a property manager may have 40 percent of their bonus tied to company profitability, 50 percent allocated to their specific property profitability, and 10 percent allocated to individual goals. A manager in accounting will have perhaps 80 percent of their bonus calculated on the company goal and 20 percent on individual goals – some of which may be financial in nature, such as managing the expense of their department.

The company profitability goal is the same for everyone, and we establish a very simple range of targets for which an increasing percentage of the bonus may be earned. It is critical that all goals are as objective as possible so that, at any time, the manager can calculate what they stand to earn in annual bonus. We openly talk at each management meeting about where we stand against our targets and what percentage of our bonuses appears reachable. Candid, open, and frequent discussion is vital, coupled with goals that are not a mystery, that are not moving targets, and that cannot be manipulated by senior management.

People Make the Difference

In my opinion the word *tenant* is demeaning and antiquated. We do not have tenants; we have customers. This sounds very simple; yet this distinction sets the tone in our company and has helped us foster a culture that is very customer-service focused. Ultimately, this distinction has a significant financial impact, since it is far cheaper to retain an existing customer than move a new one in. We carefully monitor our customer retention percentage and measure it against those of our competitors. We spend a great deal of time training our people and instilling in them an ethic of customer service – it's like a religion. We've established systems to provide quick responses to customer needs, and we set up financial incentives for our property personnel, based on the ratings they receive for customer service. We have a third-party firm perform annual surveys of our customers, and we also evaluate ourselves by having our own property managers evaluate and critique each other's property.

When hiring new employees, I look for people who are highly motivated, clear-thinking, and energetic, who have a positive attitude, and who are willing to work as part of a team. Clearly, I want to see experience that can be adapted to our company, but it is important that the individual is open-minded and not wed to doing things the way they have always been done.

The one unique characteristic I look for is that the person has been through a trying experience or has suffered through the result of a poor decision and been humbled in some way. I have found these types of experiences allow people to be more adaptive, more understanding, and better team players. Humbling experiences cause people to keep their egos in check by being more cautious after having had to reassess their own decision-making capability. We all make mistakes – but I would rather have the big ones made on someone else's watch. Of course, I look for experience in the industry. I want to see that a person has been a winner and has a track record of sticking with a job or an assignment.

REITs and the Future of Real Estate Investment

The recapitalization of real estate that occurred in the early to mid-1990s has had a profound positive effect on the industry – not the recapitalization itself, but that Wall Street became the source and the interface for the bulk of the capital required to recapitalize the industry. Wall Street is a disciplined source of capital that the industry had never before seen. Quarterly reporting to the SEC, audited GAAP-based financial statements, the scrutiny of analysts and institutional investors – all have made the industry far more responsible and disciplined. That is not to say that certain markets or product types will never be overbuilt; they will be. This time, however, it will be more a function of softening of demand caused by unforeseen economic issues, as opposed to supply added because the capital was available and the developer could earn a quick fee. Excess capacity should be more "on the margin," or more modest in nature, as compared to the unprecedented capacity that was added in the 1980s and early 1990s. The capital fueling the industry today has much more accessibility to information about markets, companies, and product classes. The industry is weathering the current economic downturn quite well when compared to history, all because of the discipline dictated by the new source of capital.

The scrutiny of Wall Street was introduced with the widespread adoption of real estate investment trusts. REITs have been around for some time, but they weren't widely used until the recapitalization of the industry. REITs now own about the same amount of institutional real estate as pension funds. Together, it is estimated that they control roughly 75 percent of institutional-quality real estate in the United States.

A publicly traded REIT offers high-quality management and a capital structure incorporating relatively low leverage, enabling it to weather difficult times, and it is subject to financial reporting requirements, just as any other public company. Almost every property category has been explored by REITs: hotels, resorts, retail, industrial, land developments, mobile home parks, senior housing, and more. Some REITs are defined geographically; some are defined by product type; and some by both criteria.

Investors are now offered the opportunity to invest in very high-quality properties managed by experienced management teams. These stocks offer quarterly cash distributions or dividends, as well as appreciation based on the values of the underlying real estate owned. REITs are particularly attractive in an environment in which the stock market is uncertain, given their significant cash flow backed by real assets.

The 1990s was a successful period for REITs, establishing them as a significant force in the real estate industry. It is important, however, that both REITs and the real estate industry not overlook the continued influence that pension fund capital has on the industry. With $8 trillion in assets, pension funds are potentially a far bigger force in impacting the industry over the near term than REITs. The industry and REITs themselves need to do a better job of courting pension-fund capital. It is my belief that, in time, pension funds will allocate a greater percentage of their total portfolios to real estate and that a growing percentage of that allocation may go to REIT stocks, as opposed to direct investments in real estate. Either way, REITs will benefit.

Another change I foresee is that more real estate companies will be run by financial, investment, and operating professionals who have no previous real estate experience. This will bring a fresh perspective and interesting changes to the industry. We already have such professionals in our company. The industry will continue to be more institutionalized, with improved reporting and disclosure. REITs are now represented in the S&P 500, increasing their appeal to a broader institutional audience.

Real estate is among the largest industries in the U.S., representing more than 27 percent of the GDP. As an investment alternative, it should not be ignored, and, with its recent recapitalization, it can be a very defensive investment alternative. This change is nothing new; Australia and much of Europe have already made this transition successfully.

John C. Goff is vice chairman and chief executive officer of Crescent Real Estate Equities Company, one of the largest publicly traded real estate investment trusts in the U.S., with more than $4 billion in assets. Upon cofounding Crescent in the early 1990s, Mr. Goff served as CEO through its initial public offering in May 1994 until December 1996, when he became vice chairman of the Board of Trust Managers. He returned as CEO in June 1999.

Mr. Goff joined Rainwater, Inc., in 1987, shortly after Richard E. Rainwater began the company as a private investor. From 1987 to 1994, Mr. Goff was vice president of Rainwater, Inc., serving as senior investment advisor and principal. Mr. Goff was responsible for Mr.

Rainwater's foray into real estate, designing the strategy and acquiring the assets that led to the initial public offering of Crescent.

Mr. Goff is the managing principal of Goff Moore Strategic Partners, L.P. (GMSP), a private investment partnership. The partnership focuses on investments outside the scope of Crescent and is currently involved in the management of more than $1 billion in assets.

From 1981 to 1987 Mr. Goff was employed by KPMG Peat Marwick, with Mr. Rainwater as one of his principal clients. Before joining KPMG Peat Marwick, Mr. Goff was employed by Century Development Corporation, a major office developer and property management company.

In addition to Crescent, Mr. Goff serves on the boards of Gainsco, Inc., The Staubach Company, OpenConnect Systems, Inc., Texas Capital Bancshares, Inc., and the National Association of Real Estate Investment Trusts (NAREIT).

REAL ESTATE – A NEW ERA

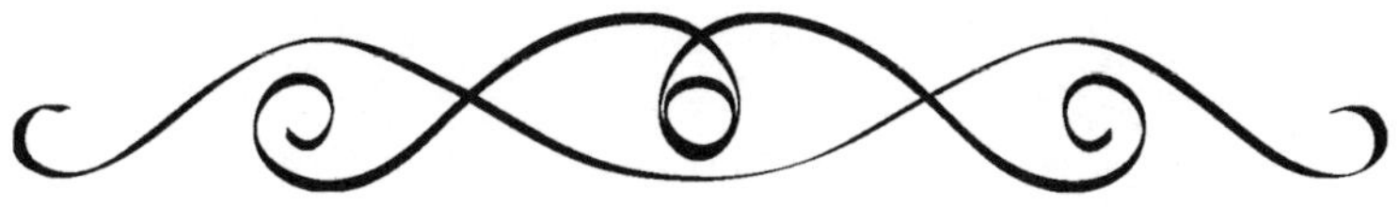

GLENN J. RUFRANO

New Plan Excel Realty Trust, Inc.

Chief Executive Officer

Real Estate Industry Trends

When I look at the real estate industry, I see a couple of significant trends. When public companies started, there were groups of assets that entrepreneurs put together, but now the biggest challenge is running a real estate company in the model of a corporate public company. We have to conform to the investment horizons in the public arena. We have to report quarterly, not think only five years in advance. We have to report the way other public companies report, have to have credible management and clear strategies. The most difficult challenge is to move from a collection of assets to a business with a longer-term strategy that can articulate performance on a quarterly basis.

All real estate companies are capital intensive. We require capital to grow by either renovating our existing assets or buying and creating new assets. All capital requires liquidity or perceived liquidity. No one wants to tie up capital for a long term without knowing how to liquefy.

Those two concepts become the basis for the model of the future. The model of the future involves larger public companies that own real estate, which will be able to attract both public and private capital. The larger public company has a float in its stock and its debt, so investors can supply capital, and if they so choose, accomplish liquidity goals by selling securities. A large public company provides a great conduit for capital and resulting liquidity.

A small private company ($1 billion to $2 billion in assets) can do the same thing. You can scoop up capital from private investors. The liquidity comes in the form of selling assets. Opportunity funds buy and sell assets with return to investors, and if they do a good job, they'll always get more capital. The two models that don't work well are the smaller public company, because you don't have the liquidity, or the large private company, because you are selling assets, thereby creating smaller companies.

Over the next five years these two models will become more effective. Smaller private companies with higher-return investments will be run by entrepreneurs who have sources of capital they have invested and made money with. The larger public companies will be larger and will have moderate-return investments, a more diversified portfolio, and higher-quality management, with systems in place that will make them extremely competitive in the long term.

In looking to the future of the real estate industry, we should expect better dissemination of information. This is beginning to occur because of the transparency in public companies and better general communication via the Internet – and the industry is better able to police itself because of this information. As a result there will be fewer cyclical problems, and we'll be able to manage ourselves in such a way as to deal with reasonable cycles.

If I could change one thing about this industry, I would change the negative reputation our industry has suffered; over time I think this is changing.

Strategy and Execution

Change is inevitable – what works today may not work tomorrow. In the smaller, private model you can be very nimble because you are buying and selling assets. Change becomes less problematic because you are working through a cycle. If you are a larger company and not selling and buying assets as frequently, then change becomes extremely important to plan for.

The way I believe you can plan for that change is through diversification. You have to have a level of diversification in tenant base, geography, and prudent leverage, so that at any given time, no single change can knock you out. The national exposure of diversification provides opportunity. If you limit your property type to community shopping centers, such as we have, and you limit your leverage to a certain level, then the only way to be opportunistic is to be geographically national. What you do not want to do is limit your leverage, your geography, and your property type. We want to leave at least one of them open for optimistic investing.

To continue to be successful, you have to have a strategy for the company over the next five years. Every day you should you know the plan you are moving toward for the five years. Then there's execution. You must support those ideas within your strategy. Having a strategy without execution is meaningless: you don't have a five-year plan; you have a day-to-day plan. Executing on a longer-term plan allows us to move toward a goal.

Trying to run a company day-to-day and stay on top of the trends is hard. As a leader, your management style must involve delegation. You have to have qualified people to delegate to. You can set the stage for the operating plan and the vision, and others can execute the vision. After this, the CEO can be free to do whatever else needs to be done, which means to be part of the marketplace. You have to get out with your constituencies. I have to be out with my tenants and understand them; I have to meet with our employees; and I have to relate to our shareholders to comprehend the trends that are affecting them.

Real estate is local by nature. If you are geographically diversified, your management challenges are enormous. You need to create a management team and a model that can manage a national portfolio, but at the same time, it must be local in the understanding of the market, so the properties can be managed on a local basis.

As a CEO, I think it is very important to be clear on the vision of the company (its mission statement). The people in the company have to be clear on their participation in that mission statement. People are more important to the company than your real estate. You can own the best real estate in the world, but you have to have a staff of qualified people who can run the real estate. Real estate is not only capital-intensive, but it is also management-intensive. And you have to lead by example, meeting three requirements: You must be honest and smart, and you must work hard.

Calculating Risk and Income

Real estate planning has to match the investors' requirements and expectations against that which can be provided by the company's assets. A company has shareholders, employees, and tenants. You have to satisfy all three. On the shareholder side, from the capital standpoint, there is a risk level, and shareholders must know what we can provide in terms of returns when they invest. In our business we tell our investors we will have a well-diversified asset base, geographically and from a tenant standpoint, and we will have prudent or low leverage.

I look at risk in terms of math. Standard deviation and probability theory show how risk is determined. Risk is defined as the probability of loss. If you accept that as risk, then what we care about is not losing money. In the case of a 100 percent deviation to return, I could lose money. If I have 4 percent or 5 percent standard deviation to return, I could lose less money, so it is less risky. If we were going to buy an investment in an opportunity fund, a business I was in prior to my current position, and we had a 20 percent investment return requirement over two to five years, the standard deviation for that could be 20 percent, which could mean we might make 0 or 40 percent. Where we are now in our plan, we are not taking that risk. On a single-asset basis we are buying returns at 11 percent to 14 percent, and the standard deviation is no more than 4 percent or 5 percent. Our investors are not looking for a 20 percent deviation.

The other part of risk mitigation is portfolio diversification. People are starting to think about portfolio risk rather than single-asset risk in real estate, which is the way it should be. In an international opportunity fund, you have portfolios of properties invested around the world – with the de-linkage of economies, there should be no two places in the world where investment return should be zero at the same time. You may lose in Argentina, but win big in Europe. The portfolio concept is important in both the middle- and high-risk arena. If we are buying all over North America and augmenting this geographic diversification with tenant diversification, and there are no tenants that could cause a problem, this reduces our standard deviation in the portfolio, reducing our risk.

We work in a business where base rent, our primary source of income, is fixed for various portions of time, usually between two and 10 years. You can calculate this income from many of our properties. The first place you need to start is at the property level. We have more than 300 properties, and for each property we have a lease-by-lease analysis, estimating what the properties will provide in five years of income. Once you have this property analysis, you can roll it up into corporate models. This model has the profit and loss statement of the properties. We can look at our projected P&L on a five-year basis and our balance sheet capitalization. We can take a look at the relationship between debt and equity, coupled with the detailed analysis, to provide the risk levels to be expected by our investors. We can see how to squeeze the balance sheet, so we can have the lowest cost relative to the return on equity on the top line. It's the combination of going from the single tenant to the five-year corporate balance sheet that gives us a planning method for going forward and allows us to look at the diversification analysis by tenant and geography. If we see any of those levels getting too high, we can sell out of a market entirely or sell out or reduce a tenant.

Balancing Supply and Demand

We look at supply and demand first by geography and property type. From 1995 through 2000 we had wonderful supply and demand parameters. We had problems around 1986 in real estate, and by 1991 we were in a depression in real estate. Although you can also apply the numbers to other property types, in retail we have today about 45,000 retail properties in the country, totaling about 5.7 billion square feet. From 1986 to 1990 we were increasing the inventory of space by about 5 percent a year, so we were building at a rate of 5 percent a year. Sales being generated by those retail properties were growing at 2 percent a year. This reveals a disaster approaching, because this means merchants were losing market share. From 1991 to 1993 we were in a huge retail depression. These numbers were similar in scale for office, industrial, hotels, and residential. From 1991 to 1995 the retail properties were growing at 2 percent a year, but sales were growing at 3.5 percent. We were setting the stage for a more balanced five-year period. From 1995 to 2000 there was a wonderful market in fundamentals, and in retail we were increasing space at only 2 percent a year, but sales were increasing at 6.5 percent a year.

We are now at another junction. In 2001 we were still growing at only 2 percent, but sales went from 6.5 percent down to 3 percent. That's partly due to September 11 and the poor economic climate we are in. We are starting to see equilibrium set in, and as a result, anytime sales drop that much, there is fallout. There are numerous tenants who have not been able to deal with sales volumes that have been halved. Our fundamentals revolve around supply and demand, and when you dig through supply and demand by property type and by geography, you will find a predictable indicator of the future.

On top of the supply-and-demand characteristics, the factors that are important are the underlying principles behind supply and demand: GDP growth, inflation, and unemployment.

Business Advice

The best advice I ever received was "Don't fall in love with the real estate." This relates to the theory of change, because you could fall in love with a piece of real estate, and some form of change will cause physical or economic absorbance. If you're blinded by love, you will never see it.

To be successful in real estate, you have to follow the three golden rules:

1. Know the fundamentals of your properties, and understand their market position and their trends. Don't let any of the details go untended.
2. Recognize that portfolios are more valuable than single assets.

3. When dealing with investors, don't oversell your position. It's better for them to "watch what you do, not what you say," when selling a position.

Glenn J. Rufrano joined New Plan Excel Realty Trust in February 2000, following 17 years as a partner at The O'Connor Group, a diversified real estate investment firm. In his final position at The O'Connor Group, he served as president and chief operating officer, overseeing the investment and management of three private equity funds, in addition to client service and marketing and finance activities. Concurrently, he was co-chairman of The Peabody Group, an association between The O'Connor Group and J.P. Morgan & Co., Inc., investing in high-yield international real estate related opportunities.

Early in his career Mr. Rufrano was a senior vice president in the Appraisal and Property Dispositions Department at Landauer Associates. He currently serves on a number of boards at New York University's Real Estate Institute, where he is an adjunct professor, and is a member of the

Board of Directors of TrizecHahn Corporation, an integrated real estate operating company. Additionally, Mr. Rufrano is an active member of the Urban Land Institute, the International Council of Shopping Centers, and the Pension Real Estate Association.

Mr. Rufrano holds an MSM from Florida International University and a BA from Rutgers University. He lives in Bellmore, New York.

FROM OPPORTUNITY TO EXECUTION

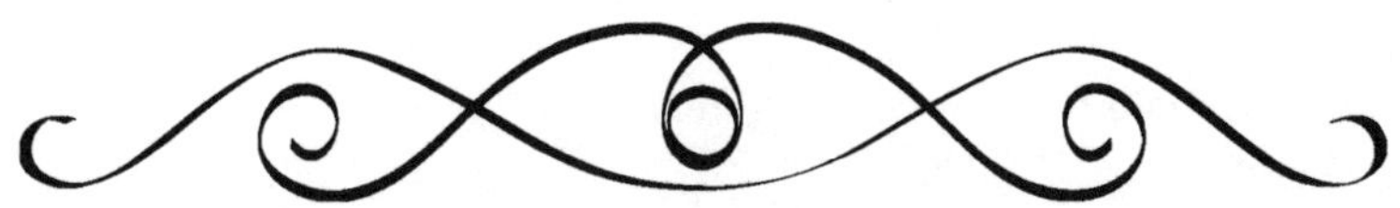

STEVEN J. GUTTMAN

Federal Realty Investment Trust

Chairman and Chief Executive Officer

Finding That Sense of Place

When considering a development project, the first thing we do is assess the need for additional retail or residential space in the market. Ours is a fairly narrow sliver of the real estate industry – we specialize in retail development, focusing on urban mixed-use development and the creation of pedestrian-friendly environments. If there is no need for a specific kind of retail or residential activity, then we have no interest in doing it.

Right now, for example, we're engaged in a large-scale development in San Jose, California, where we think there is a definite need for a sense of place to be created. In San Jose there is no restaurant district, no entertainment district; the city had a big void, and we believe we're helping to fill that void. We spot opportunities by looking at what is lacking in people's lives: What do they like doing? How do they want to spend time? Do they enjoy shopping in an enclosed mall, or are they shopping there out of necessity? Is Wal-Mart serving the constituency well, or are people looking for something a little different? Our goal is to create lasting places. Is there a need for what a property delivers? Is the location special and unique enough that it will continue to do well over time?

Once you spot an opportunity, you have to organize it so that it's as interesting and effective as it can be. What's the plan of the property? Will it be a neighborhood shopping center or a Main Street environment? Regardless of what type of environment it will be, the main ingredients have to be there. The project has to have easy access, convenient parking, wide sidewalks, and a strong architectural design. If you do not have those essential elements, you do not have anything to start with.

Once you have the basics, you want to focus on merchandising – creating a retail and restaurant mix that is otherwise lacking in the area. Your goal should be to meet a need in the area and create an interesting and dynamic environment.

I find development and creation to be the most exciting aspects. It excites me to create an environment that works, that people enjoy, and that is vibrant and profitable. To take a piece of raw land, or an under-used retail district, and transform either into a frequently visited, pedestrian-friendly environment is tremendously rewarding.

We focus primarily on locations where there is a high density of people, a significant supply constraint, and not a lot of vacant properties in the district. We want a location that is very precious, providing the opportunity to achieve something that is important to the community. We want to create value for the investors. At the conclusion of a development, the goal is to look back at the investment and feel that significant value has been created.

Creating value takes time, as the development life cycle, particularly for complex projects, can be long. Generally here are the steps we follow:

1. Secure the property.
2. Go through the zoning process, which can take upwards of two years.

3. Go through the process of developing the plans and specifications of the property and the plan review, which can take six months to three years.
4. Begin construction, which is a one- to two-year process.
5. Get the property stabilized, which can take three to 18 months.

Risk and the Economy

When it comes to assessing investment risk, I have a longer-term time horizon than many real estate developers. I look at risk over a 10- or 20-year period, not over a three-year period, and try to determine whether the property will become better over 10 to 20 years and do better every year by a significant margin. By measuring risk in that way, you eliminate one part of the risk element.

The unanswerable question is this: If you're building things that cannot be pre-leased effectively, how do you eliminate the risk of an adverse change in the national economy? Anytime you are undertaking a development project that will take five to seven years to complete, you may have severe fluctuations in the economy during that time. You have to get capital affiliated with you that helps you navigate through those risks and that has the same time horizon.

The biggest variable is the local and national economy. If you're developing a power center, you don't have to worry, but we are passionate about doing special, unique properties that are unfortunately more subject to the fluctuations in the national economy.

Future Opportunities

In the future, I believe there will be a growing trend for specialization because the industry has a wide spectrum of talent: financial people, construction people, office people, leasing people, accounting types. As the industry has matured, there has also been a growing level of professionalism. Many business and graduate schools teach real estate.

In the next five to 10 years, I think big companies will get bigger and dominate certain areas of investments, but they will also leave room for others to pursue smaller investments that don't fit the scale of a big company. Also, as real estate companies get bigger, they become less agile and entrepreneurial, and that creates opportunities for individual investors, as well.

Right now, construction lenders discourage creativity because unless there is a precedent for a particular type of building, they would rather the activity not happen. If lenders were a little more prepared under the circumstances to have vision, then society would be rewarded with more interesting architecture and more interesting products. It is very hard for anyone to build anything new or different or innovative. You have to take baby steps, or you cannot get it financed. As a result, everyone is building the same things everywhere.

Succeeding as a Leader in Real Estate

The most important quality the CEO of a development company can have is the ability to provide leadership and vision. As a leader, you should try to select the opportunities that are most compelling for the company, based on where you can best serve your various constituencies. Being a good leader takes communication. Ask yourself: Do you communicate effectively with your team? Do they understand the mission well enough to execute it?

To ensure effective execution, I communicate with people through frequent interfaces. If you meet on a regular basis and hit on most of the issues, and you have an engaged team that challenges you and each other, then you can quickly identify where the ball is slipping away from you. I always stress the importance of what we are doing and the necessity of working together as a team, and emphasize how the project is a special opportunity. How we execute matters to us, to our investors, and to the community.

I'm personally a very hands-on, detail-oriented leader. I pay attention to the details I care about, and I like smaller-group environments. I try to encourage innovation within my company by thinking "outside the box" myself and by leading by example. Innovation is critical in the real estate industry because it allows you to get a jumpstart on the competition by having systems that are more integrated, smoother, and faster than the competition.

To make sure the company will be successful over the long term, you need a sustaining asset base. Then you need a talent and people base that provides the necessary expertise and commitment. A company should succeed if it has a group of individuals who are talented and committed to maximizing the asset base that has been assembled and enhancing it over time.

If you follow these "golden rules" of the real estate industry, you should be quite successful:

1. Pick the right location.
2. Finance it intelligently.
3. Execute the development as well as it can be executed.

4. Create the infrastructure so it can be managed, leased, and operated to achieve maximum efficiency and profitability.

Steven J. Guttman is chairman and chief executive officer of Federal Realty Investment Trust and serves on the company's Board of Trustees. Mr. Guttman joined the Trust in 1972. In 1975 he became director of acquisitions and was promoted to chief operating officer. He became managing trustee in 1979 and was elected president, chief executive officer, and trustee in 1980, the position he currently holds.

Mr. Guttman is currently serving his third term on the Board of Governors of the National Association of Real Estate Investment Trusts, where he also served as chairman and member of the Executive Committee. He has held active membership in the International Council of Shopping Centers since 1972 and served as trustee from 1991 to 1997. Mr. Guttman is also a member of the Real Estate Center Advisory Board of the Wharton School of the

University of Pennsylvania, is a member of the Executive Committee, and is chairman of the Membership/Program Committee. Additionally, he is a member of the Board of Advisors of the George Washington University Law School.

Mr. Guttman graduated with honors from the University of Pittsburgh. He has a law degree from George Washington University in Washington, D.C., where he graduated with honors.

Other Books, Briefs & Journals Published By Aspatore

Business Travel Bible™ (BTB) - *A* Permanent Fixture in Every Business Traveler's Briefcase/Suitcase - Every phone number (both listed and unlisted) for all airlines, hotels, car rentals and other frequently used services, Business travel emergencies (your computer crashes, you get sick, you lose your plane ticket, wallet, etc.) and what to do, Business words and phrases in the 14 most common foreign languages, and spelled out phonetically, Maps of the 23 Biggest U.S. Cities for Business, Business resource directory for computer support, pda & cell phone assistance, credit card companies, banks, shipping locations, impromptu meeting locations, Information on roadside assistance, local ISP #s, hospitals/health resources, local taxi and transportation information and more... $19.95

ExecRecs™ - *Executive Recommendations For The Best Products, Services & Intelligence Executives Use to Excel* - Recommendations on Best Business Books, Favorite PDA, Favorite Airline, Best Business Advice for Upcoming Year and Much, Much More…"The Zagat® equivalent for business professionals." – Robyn Sachs, RMR & Assoc., CEO $14.95

The Business Translator - Business to-do's and not to-do's for all major countries and ethnicities for traveling abroad or doing business with international business professionals in the U.S. Hundreds of business words and phrases in 90 different languages, all spelled out phonetically so you can pronounce them. A must have for anyone traveling internationally or doing business with international business executives in the U.S. $29.95

What Ifs™ - What ifs is a journal designed to enable business professionals to prepare for the unexpected. The journal features question blocks on topics such as human resources, financials, customers, competitors, partners, and technology, with lined spaces for you to put your answers. Sample questions include: "What if I lose my biggest customer/client?" "What if my most important employee quits?" "What if my competitor cuts their prices in half?" "What if we can no longer offer our biggest selling product/service?" Each page contains a different question, with lines to fill in your answers. Executives and managers at every level should have one of these filled out and ready to go just in case a "What If" scenario occurs. $14.95

Brainstormers™ - Brainstormers™ question blocks and idea-development worksheets are designed by leading business executives as the most efficient way to generate new ideas, develop them, and then execute and bring those ideas to fruition. Too many ideas vanish on pieces of scratch paper or don't even make it to paper before getting lost among the myriad thoughts in a person's mind. Brainstormers™ are an effective way to stimulate your mind to think in new ways and to centralize your ideas, whether for an entirely new product or service, a way to increase efficiencies, profits, or internal teamwork, or even just a way to do something differently. Each page contains a different question, with lines to fill in your answers. Management Brainstormers™, Marketing Brainstormers™, Technology Brainstormers™, Entrepreneurial Brainstormers™, Law Brainstormers™ $14.95 Each

---

CareerJournal™ - The CareerJournal™ was developed by leading business executives as the most efficient way to remember key situations, learn from them, and plan for the future. Too many times during the busy course of weeks, months, and years, key events are forgotten, follow-up with contacts and mentors is neglected, and goals are not set. The CareerJournal™ is a way to centralize your thoughts, maintain your contacts, and set goals for your future -- regardless of the current stage of your career. In addition, the CareerJournal™ serves as a timeless reference you can use to collect your ideas and memories throughout the course of your career. Don't let another key event, observation, or job pass you by with out recording it in your CareerJournal™. You never know when it may be useful. Evaluate, plan, and excel with your CareerJournal™. Only $29.95

IdeaJournal™ - The IdeaJournal™ was developed by leading business executives, politicians, and lawyers as the most efficient way to generate new ideas, develop them, and then execute and bring those ideas to fruition. Too many ideas vanish on pieces of scratch paper or don't even make it onto paper before getting lost among the myriad thoughts in a person's mind. The IdeaJournal™ is an effective way to centralize all your ideas, whether for an entirely new product or service, a way to increase efficiencies, profits, or internal teamwork, or even just a different way to do something. In addition, the IdeaJournal™ can serve as a timeless reference; ideas that you may not be able to use now could be helpful in the future. Don't let another idea pass you by with out recording it in your IdeaJournal™. You never know when it may be useful. Start capitalizing on your ideas with the IdeaJournal™. Only $29.95

The Focusbook™ - Assemble Your Own Business Book - Ever wish you could assemble your own business book, and even add your own thoughts in the book? Here is your chance to become the managing editor or your own book! The Focusbook™ enables you to become the managing editor of your own book, by selecting individual chapters from the best selling business books published by Aspatore Books to assemble your own business book. A Focusbook™ can highlight a particular topic, industry, or area of expertise for yourself, your team, your course, or even your entire company. You can even add additional text of your own to the book, such as reference information, points to focus on, or even a course syllabus, in order to further customize it to better suit your needs. The Focusbook™ is the future of business books, allowing you to become the managing editor of your own business book, based on what you deem important, enabling yourself, and others to focus, innovate and outperform.

Inside the Minds: Leading Litigators-Litigation Chairs Revel the Secrets to the Art & Science of Litigation (ISBN: 1587621592)
Inside the Minds: Leading IP Lawyers-IP Chairs Reveal the Secrets to the Art & Science of IP Law (ISBN: 1587621606)
Inside the Minds: Leading Deal Makers-Negotiations, Leveraging Your Position and the Art of Deal Making (ISBN: 1587620588)
Inside the Minds: Internet Lawyers-Important Answers to Issues For Every Entrepreneur, Lawyer & Anyone With a Web Site (ISBN: 1587620065)
Bigwig Briefs: The Art of Deal Making-The Secrets to the Deal Making Process (ISBN: 1587621002)
Bigwig Briefs: Career Options for Law School Students-Leading Partners Reveal the Secrets to Choosing the Best Career Path (ISBN: 1587621010)

MARKETING/ADVERTISING/PR

Inside the Minds: Leading Marketers-Leading Chief Marketing Officers Reveal the Secrets to Building a Billion Dollar Brand (ISBN: 1587620537)
Inside the Minds: Leading Advertisers-Advertising CEOs Reveal the Tricks of the Advertising Profession (ISBN: 1587620545)
Inside the Minds: The Art of PR-Leading PR CEOs Reveal the Secrets to the Public Relations Profession (ISBN: 1587620634)
Inside the Minds: PR Visionaries-The Golden Rules of PR and Becoming a Senior Level Advisor With Your Clients (ISBN: 1587621517)
Bigwig Briefs: Guerrilla Marketing -The Best of Guerrilla Marketing-Big Marketing Ideas For a Small Budget (ISBN: 1587620677)
Bigwig Briefs: Become a VP of Marketing-How to Get There, Stay There, and Empower Others That Work With You (ISBN: 1587620707)

FINANCIAL

Inside the Minds: Leading Accountants-The Golden Rules of Accounting & the Future of the Accounting Industry and Profession (ISBN: 1587620529)
Inside the Minds: The Financial Services Industry-The Future of the Financial Services Industry & Professions (ISBN: 1587620626)
Inside the Minds: Leading Investment Bankers-Leading I-Bankers Reveal the Secrets to the Art & Science of Investment Banking (ISBN: 1587620618)
Bigwig Briefs: Become a CFO-Leading CFOs Reveal How to Get There, Stay There, and Empower Others That Work With You (ISBN: 1587620731)
Bigwig Briefs: Become a VP of Biz Dev-How to Get There, Stay There, and Empower Others That Work With You (ISBN: 1587620723)
Bigwig Briefs: Career Options for MBAs-I-Bankers, Consultants & CEOs Reveal the Secrets to Choosing the Best Career Path (ISBN: 1587621029)

INVESTING

Inside the Minds: Building a $1,000,000 Nest Egg -Simple, Proven Ways for Anyone to Build a $1M Nest Egg On Your Own Terms (ISBN: 1587622157)
Inside the Minds: Leading Wall St. Investors-The Best Investors of Wall Street Reveal the Secrets to Profiting in Any Economy (ISBN: 1587621142)

FOR A FULL LIST OF TITLES, VISIT WWW.ASPATORE.COM

INSIDE THE MINDS:

THE REAL ESTATE INDUSTRY

Acknowledgements and Dedications

Mitchell E. Hersh
This chapter is dedicated to my late father, Bernard Hersh, the person and professional I emulated.

William T. Atkins
In this chapter I borrowed liberally from two of my heroes: Tom Peters and David Birch. In the 1980s these two, together with several others, pointed out to me the convergence of the trends discussed here. It was partly their courage to question conventional wisdom that emboldened me to help create a real estate company that has for years ignored the historical rhetoric in the industry and pioneered a new small-tenant office product. Based on service and focused on this fast-growing but neglected market segment, AmeriVest Properties Inc. has recently been recognized as one of the fastest growing REITs in the country and has been able to reward its shareholders with one of the highest total returns in the industry. I must thank our many shareholders whose support has made the company's success possible.

Several people contributed to this chapter who deserve to be recognized: Charles Knight, John Greenman, and Sandy Hewitt at AmeriVest; Mark Decker at Ferris, Baker Watts; my father, who taught me most of what I know, and my children – Marie, Katherine, Victor, and Tess – who give me certainty that the future will be a better place.

ASPATORE
C-Level Business Intelligence™